IT'S TIME TO LEARN ABOUT FLYING BATS

It's Time to Learn about Flying Bats

Walter the Educator

Silent King Books
A WhichHead Entertainment Imprint

Copyright © 2025 by Walter the Educator

All rights reserved. No part of this book may be reproduced in any manner whatsoever without written per- mission except in the case of brief quotations embodied in critical articles and reviews.

First Printing, 2024

Disclaimer

This book is a literary work; the story is not about specific persons, locations, situations, and/or circumstances unless mentioned in a historical context. Any resemblance to real persons, locations, situations, and/or circumstances is coincidental. This book is for entertainment and informational purposes only. The author and publisher offer this information without warranties expressed or implied. No matter the grounds, neither the author nor the publisher will be accountable for any losses, injuries, or other damages caused by the reader's use of this book. The use of this book acknowledges an understanding and acceptance of this disclaimer.

It's Time to Learn about Flying Bats is a collectible early learning book by Walter the Educator suitable for all ages belonging to Walter the Educator's Time to Eat Book Series. Collect more books at WaltertheEducator.com

USE THE EXTRA SPACE TO TAKE NOTES AND DOCUMENT YOUR MEMORIES

FLYING BATS

When the sun sets and the sky turns black,

It's Time to Learn about Flying Bats

The flying bats wake up and snack.

With flapping wings, they swoop and glide,

Through trees and caves, they race and hide.

A bat's not a bird, but it flies so high,

It flaps its wings across the sky.

With tiny claws, it hangs so tight,

Upside down all through the night!

Some bats are big, some bats are small,

Some love to chirp, some barely call.

But every bat, both near and far,

Knows just where the insects are!

They use their ears to find their way,

Even in the darkest gray.

A sound goes out, a sound comes back,

That helps them fly and stay on track!

It's Time to Learn about
Flying Bats

Most bats love bugs, they catch them fast,

They zoom and swoop as they fly past.

With open mouths, they chomp and chew,

Mosquitoes, moths, and beetles too!

Some bats drink fruit juice so sweet,

They munch on mangoes for a treat.

They help new plants grow big and tall,

By spreading seeds when fruits do fall.

Bats live in caves, in trees, in barns,

In jungle lands and fields and farms.

They rest all day and sleep so tight,

Then wake and soar into the night.

Their wings are thin, like stretched-out skin,

With tiny bones tucked deep within.

So when they glide, they twist and turn,

It's Time to Learn about
Flying Bats

A special skill they had to learn!

Bats help the world in many ways,

By eating bugs and spreading sprays.

They keep the farms and gardens neat,

And help grow food that we all eat!

So if you see a bat at night,

Don't be scared, it won't take flight

To chase you down or cause you fear,

It's Time to Learn about
Flying Bats

It's just a friend that's flying near!

ABOUT THE CREATOR

Walter the Educator is one of the pseudonyms for Walter Anderson. Formally educated in Chemistry, Business, and Education, he is an educator, an author, a diverse entrepreneur, and he is the son of a disabled war veteran. "Walter the Educator" shares his time between educating and creating. He holds interests and owns several creative projects that entertain, enlighten, enhance, and educate, hoping to inspire and motivate you. Follow, find new works, and stay up to date with Walter the Educator™ at WaltertheEducator.com

www.ingramcontent.com/pod-product-compliance
Lightning Source LLC
LaVergne TN
LVHW051920060526
838201LV00060B/4104